Laugh Your Socks Off Jokes for Kids Aged 5-7

500+ Awesome Jokes Guaranteed to Make You Laugh Out Loud!

Laughing Lion

Free **Audiobook versions** of this and many other Laughing Lion books?
Sign up using the link below or scan the QR code with your phone.

bit.ly/3j3vmD2

Can a normal morning breakfast be funny? How about a long day at school? Are some days really just boring, or can everyday actually be a chance to laugh until your tummy hurts?

Laugh Your Socks Off is a collection of fun and whacky jokes you can read and share with others wherever you go. Each chapter takes you to a different world where you'd find animals poking fun at each other, plants with witty one-liners, and magical creatures who tell the craziest knock-knock jokes!

So, if you're looking for a whimsical and absolutely hilarious journey, this book is for you. May it take you, your family, and your friends on a fun road trip and remind you that you can find laughter and joy anywhere, if you look hard enough.

CONTENTS

RISE AND SHINE

♦ • ♦ • ♦ • ♦ • ♦ • ♦ • ♦

Why was the broom late for school?

It over-swept!

How do eggs feel every morning?
Egg-cited!

Mom: "Knock, knock!"
Timmy: "Who's there?"
Mom: "I'm Soup."
Timmy: "I'm Soup who?"
Mom: "I'm Soupermom! I just made you breakfast!"

What did the cup of coffee say to the cup of tea?
"I really like you a LATTE!"

Why did the boy throw a stick of butter out the window?
He wanted to see a butter fly!

Why was the strawberry crying?
Because they're in a jam!

What is a cat's favorite breakfast?
Mice Crispies!

What did the plate say to the drinking glass?
"Breakfast is on me!"

Why did the cookie call for a doctor?
He felt really crummy!

Dad: "Knock, knock!"
Mom: "Who's there?"
Dad: "Omelet."
Mom: "Omelet who?"
Dad: "Omelet'in you kiss me!"

Dad: "Good morning, Charlie! What do you want for breakfast?"
Charlie: "Hammond!"
Dad: "Huh?"
Charlie: "Hammond eggs for me please!"

A happy slice of cheese found one of her friends sad.

Happy cheese: "Aw, it will be okay! Everything is GOUDA!"
Sad cheese: "But I can't stop being so BLUE!"

Cat: "Did you see anything in the kitchen?"
Dog: "Luke."
Cat: "Luke? None of the humans are named Luke."
Dog: "I meant Luke! Luke at all the food!"

Boy: "Knock, knock!"
Mom: "Who's there?"
Boy: "Philip."
Mom: "Philip who?"
Boy: "Philip up my glass please, I'm thirsty!"

Duck: "Knock, knock!"
Chicken: "Who's there?"
Duck: "Aida."
Chicken: "Aida who?"
Duck: "Aida sandwich for lunch today!"

Dad: "Honey! Why are you choking that vegetable?"
Mom: "We need artichokes for this meal!"

A crocodile went over to the bird's house.

Crocodile: "Knock, knock!"
Bird: "Who's there?"
Crocodile: "Arthur."
Bird: "Arthur who?"
Crocodile: "Arthur any more cookies?"

"I'll cook the pancakes this morning!"
Tom told his mom rather FLIP-pantly.

A fox sat next to a bunny during breakfast.

Bunny: "Hi! What's your name?"
Fox: "Ada."
Bunny: "Wow! What's that short for?"
Fox: "ADA-lot for breakfast and now I'm going to throw up!"

Mummy: "I put legs in the cereal, honey! It gives you a little kick, huh?"
Zombie: "Not just that! It's chasing the dog now!"

A cookie spent breakfast saying, "I'm a cookie, I'm a cookie, I'm a cookie."
Nina saw him and told him to be quiet. She poked him right in the middle.
The cookie looked at his stomach and smiled.

"I'm a donut, I'm a donut, I'm a donut."

Vampire: "Hi, Ghost! Can you help me make a milk shake?"
Ghost: *turns to milk* "BOO!!!"
Milk: "OH MY!" *shakes*

Muffin: "I heard the new pastry's a plain bagel."
Raisin bread: "Wow, I wish I could fly, too!"

What breakfast did the cheerleader prepare for her mom?
Cheerios!

Corn: "You! Pass the butter to me."
Pea: "What's the magic word?"
Corn: *sigh* "PEAS pass the butter to me!"

Dad: "Did you hear the news about McDonalds?"
Mom: "Yes! They eggs-panded their breakfast menu!"

There are two bread slices in the toaster.
One bread slice turns to the other slice and says, "Man, it's hot in here."
The other bread slice says, "OH MY GOD A TALKING BREAD SLICE."

Tangerine: "Knock, knock!"
Apple: "Who's there?"
Tangerine: "Orange."
Apple: "Orange who?"
Tangerine: "Orange you glad to see me?"

Jake: "Dad, is it okay to eat bugs?"
Dad: "That's disgusting, son! We don't talk like that while eating."

After a few minutes, Dad was finished eating.

Dad: "Now, son, what did you want to ask me again?"
Jake: "Oh, it was nothing. There was a bug in your soup, but you seemed to enjoy it."

A dish was placed behind a drinking glass in the sink.

Dish: "Knock, knock!"
Drinking Glass: "Who's there?"
Dish: "Dishes."
Drinking Glass: "Dishes who?"
Dish: "Dishes me, who are you?"

Who stole the soap from the bath?
It's the robber ducks!

A rubber duck saw a little boy taking a bath.

Rubber duck: "Hi! What's your name?"
Boy: "Dwayne!"
Rubber duck: "Wow! What's that short for?"
Boy: "No! Dwayne the tub, I'm dwowning!"

What just gets wetter the more that it dries?
A bathroom towel!

Why should the superhero always flush the toilet?
Because it is his doody!

There was a party in the bathroom sink.

Toothbrush: "Who threw this party?"
Soap: "Razor."
Toothbrush: "Razor who?"
Soap: "Razor hands and dance the boogie!"

How can you make a tissue dance?
Put a little boogie in it!

Toilet: "Knock, knock!"
Tommy: "Who's there?"
Toilet: "Urine."
Tommy: "Urine who?"
Toilet: "Urine trouble if you don't flush!"

Why should the robot dry her feet carefully after a bath?
She might get rusty nails!

Where do hamburgers like to go dancing?
At a meat-ball!

What was the belt arrested for?
It was holding up some pants!

Two bananas in love pass by a lime and an olive.

Lime: "Did you see that, Olive?"

Olive: "My my, what a lovely pair of slippers!"

Why doesn't the lamp sink in water?

It's too light!

What did one firefly say to the lightbulb?

"You glow girl!"

Grape: "Knock, knock!"

Banana: "Who's there?"

Grape: "Juicy."

Banana: "Juicy who?"

Grape: "Juicy what I just saw?"

What did Saturday say to Sunday?

"We're the strongest days! All the others are weekdays!"

What do cows like to read in the living room?

Cattle-logs!

John: "Knock, knock!"
Sherlock: "Who's there?"
John: "Watson."
Sherlock: "Watson who?"
John: "Watson TV right now?"

Why did the lemon want to be a doctor?
So she can give some lemon aid!

What has two hands but can't clap?
A clock!

Where do horses like to live?
In NEEEIIIGH-borhoods!

What did the right eye say to the left?
"Something between us really smells!"

What kind of food does a racecar eat before a competition?
Fast Food!

What dance can rabbits and kangaroos do together?
Hip-Hop!

Ever heard the joke about the roof?
I think it will go over your head.

Why do humming birds like to hum?
They don't know the words to the song!

What kind of cheese belongs to somebody else?
Nacho cheese!

What do you get from a cow who just got off a roller coaster?
Some milkshake!

Why shouldn't you tell jokes around windows?
They might crack up!

Mailman: "Knock, knock."
Mom: "Who's there?"
Mailman: "Zany."
Mom: "Zany who?"
Mailman: "Zany body home?"

What did the buffalo say when his son left for school?
"Bison!"

Charles and Gina both need to get on the schoolbus.

Gina: "Hi! I'm Gina."
Charles: "Yugo."
Gina: "Yugo, nice to meet you!"
Charles: " I meant Yugo first, I'll be right behind you!"

LET'S GO TO THE ZOO

How did gorillas get such big nostrils?

They also have such big fingers!

What did the dog say when he sat on the sandpaper?
"Ruff!"

What's a pig that can do karate?
A pork chop!

What do porcupines say when they hug?
"Ouch!!!"

What animal likes to dress up and howl?
A wear-wolf!

Dog: "Knock, knock!"
Cat: "Who's there?"
Dog: "Poodle."
Cat: "Poodle who?"
Dog: "Poodle little bone in my bowl!"

Bird: "Knock, knock!"
Monkey: "Who's there?"
Bird: "Pecan."
Monkey: "Pecan who?"
Bird: "Pecan somebody your own size!"

Worm: "Knock, knock!"
Pigeon: "Who's there?"
Worm: "Who."
Pigeon: "Who who?"
Owl: "Are you guys making fun of me???"

Elephant: "Knock, knock!"
Lion: "Who's there?"
Elephant: "Cash."
Lion: "Cash who?"
Elephant: "No thanks, I like almonds more."

What is a kitten's favorite color?
Purrr-ple!

What's the most expensive fish in the world?
The gold fish!

What's a hen who loves to counts her eggs?
A mathemachicken!

What does the dog always press on the remote?
Paws!

Shane: "Knock, knock!"
Holly: "Who's there?"
Shane: "Manatee."
Holly: "Manatee who?"
Shane: "Manatee would be better to wear than a sweater today, it's hot!"

Sheep: "Knock knock."
Goat: "Who's there?"
Sheep: "A herd."
Goat: "A herd who?"
Sheep: "A herd you were home, so here I am!"

Snake: "Knock, knock!"
Alligator: "Who's there?"
Snake: "Althea."
Alligator: "Althea who?"
Snake: "Althea later alligator!"

Labrador: "Knock, knock!"
Dalmatian: "Who's there?"
Labrador: "Arf! Fur."
Dalmatian: "Arf! Fur who?"
Labrador: "Arf! Fur got!"

Can a kangaroo jump higher than the Burj Khalifa?
Of course! The Burj Khalifa can't jump!

Where do fish go to take care of their money?
To the riverbank!

What should you do when it rains cats and dogs?
Be careful-- you might step on a poodle!

Why doesn't the leopard like playing hide-and-seek?
He's always spotted!

Platypus: "Knock, knock!"
Otter: "Who's there?"
Platypus: "Otto."
Otter: "Really? Me too!"

Snake: "Knock, knock!"
Gorilla: "Who's there?"
Snake: "Viper."
Gorilla: "Viper who?"
Snake: "Viper nose! It's running!"

Bug: "Knock, knock!"
Bee: "Who's there?"
Bug: "Roach."
Bee: "Roach who?"
Bug: "Roach you a letter! It's on the ground. Can you read it?"

Bird: "Knock, knock!"
Johnny: "Who's There?"
Bird: "Impatient raven."
Johnny: "Impatient raven wh–"
Bird: "CAAAWWW!!!"

What do you get when a bear loses all its teeth?
A gummy bear!

Where do cows usually hang out?
The MOOOO-vies!

What's an alligator who loves solving mysteries?
An investigator!

How do bees get sticky hair?
They use honey combs!

Waiter: "What would you like, Mr. Shark?"
Shark "Two knee."
Waiter: "Pardon, Sir?"
Shark: "Two-knee fish!"

Pig: "Knock, knock!"
Chicken: "Who's there?"
Pig: "Cows go"
Chicken: "Cows go who?"
Pig: "Cows don't go who, they go MOO!"

Fish: "Knock, knock!"
Jess: "Who's there?"
Fish: "Doris."
Jess: "Doris who?"
Fish: "The Doris locked! This fish wants to come in."

Jess: *look into peephole*
"OH MY GOD! A FISH OUT OF WATER!!!"

Why is it hard to fool snakes?
Because you can't pull their leg!

What do you get when you have an evil hen?
Deviled eggs!

Why didn't tigers make good storytellers?
Because they have only one tail!

What haircut is popular with the bees?
Buzzzzzcuts!

Gloria: "Knock, knock!"

Marty: "Who's there?"

Gloria: "Hip."

Marty: "Hip who?"

Gloria: "Hippopotamus!"

Baby chick: "Knock, knock!"

Chicken: "Who's there?"

Baby chick: "Chick!"

Chicken: "Chick who?"

Baby chick: "Chick your oven, Mom! It's burning!"

Annie: "Knock, knock!"

Lucas: "Who's there?"

Annie: "Kanga."

Lucas: "Kanga who?"

Annie: "No, it's kangaROO!"

Harry: "Knock, knock!"
Rody: "Who's there?"
Harry: "Java."
Rody: "Java who?"
Harry: "Java dog in there? I can hear barking!"

Why didn't the crab want share his sweets?
He was feeling a little shellfish!

When is it bad luck to come across a black cat?
When you're a mouse!

Why do cows need to wear bells?
Because their horns won't work!

What did the snail say while it's riding on a turtle's back?
"Weeeee!!!"

Shrimp: "Knock, knock."
Pufferfish: "Who's there?"
Shrimp: "Tank."
Pufferfish: "Tank who?"
Shrimp: "You're welcome!"

Parrot: "Knock, knock!"
Mouse: "Who's there?"
Parrot: "Woo."
Mouse: "Woo who?"
Parrot: "It's nice to know that you're happy!"

Timon: "Knock, knock!"
Pumba: "Who's there?"
Timon: "Grub."
Pumba: "Grub who?"
Timon: "Grub hold of Simba! We have to go now!"

Duck: "Knock, knock."
Goose: "Who's there?"
Duck: "Quacker."
Goose: "Quacker who?"
Duck: "Quackernother bad joke and I'm leaving!"

Where do sheep like to have their wool cut?
At the BAAAA-bars!

What's black and white and blue?
A lonely panda.

What did the judge say when the skunk entered the courtroom?
"Odor in the court!"

What animal isn't fun to play games with?
A cheetah!

What day are chickens scared of?
Fry-days!

Why can't the elephant leave the airport?
They couldn't find their trunk!

Frog: "Knock, knock!"
Pig: "Who's there?"
Frog: "Kermit."
Pig: "Kermit who?"
Frog: "Kermit a crime and you'll get locked up!"

Lovebird 1: "Knock, knock!"
Lovebird 2: "Who's there?"
Lovebird 1: "Mary."
Lovebird 2: "Mary who?"
Lovebird 1: "Marry me?"

Panda: "Knock, knock!"
Elephant: "Who's there?"
Panda: A little panda
Elephant: "A little panda who?"
Panda: "A little panda who can't reach the doorbell!"

Cow: "Knock, knock!"
Horse: "Who's there?"
Cow: "Udder."
Horse: "Udder who?"
Cow: "Udder any extra hay in there? I'm hungry."

Lizard: "Knock, knock!"
Parrot: "Who's there?"
Lizard: "Cook."
Parrot: "Cook who?"
Lizard: "Yes, you kinda are!"

Goose: "Knock, knock!"
Turtle: "Who's there?"
Goose: "Goose."
Turtle: "Goose who?"
Goose: "Goose who's knocking on your shell again!"

TIME FOR SCHOOL

How do you get straight A's all the time?

Simple! Use a ruler!

Why did the teacher need sunglasses?
Her students were so bright!

What did the Math book say to the English book?
"I've got so many problems!"

Where did pencils first come from?
PENCIL-vania!

Why was the finger at the principal's office?
The nose got tired of getting picked on!

A student in a library walks up to the librarian and tells her, "I'll have a milkshake, please!"

The librarian responds, "Dear pupil, you do know you're in a library, right?"

The student says sorry, leans in and whispers,

"I'll have a milkshake, please."

Gladys: "Knock, knock!"
Rosa: "Who's there?"
Gladys: "Gladys."
Rosa: "Gladys, who?"
Gladys: "Gladys the weekend—no schoolwork!"

Neil: "There's this really cool joke about a broken pencil!"
Ace: "Whoa! How does it go?"
Neil: "Never mind, it's pointless."

Abby: "Knock, knock!"

Teacher: "Who's there?"

Abby: "Abby."

Teacher: "Abby who?"

Abby: "Abby good, just don't give me detention!"

Why are librarians so good at fishing?

Because they bring bookworms with them!

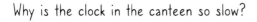

Why did the music teacher need a ladder?

So she could reach the high notes!

Why is the clock in the canteen so slow?

It always goes back four seconds!

Why didn't the sun need to go to college?

It had a million degrees already!

Macy: "Knock, knock!"

Alice: "Who's there?"

Macy: "Anita."

Alice: "Anita who?"

Macy: "Anita nother pencil! May I borrow one?"

Music Teacher: "Then one day, Beethoven gave away all his chickens."

Students: "Why?"

Music Teacher: "While he was playing, they kept calling out Bach, Bach, Bach!"

Ronald: "Teacher, I have a question!"

Teacher: "Dwight."

Ronald" "But I'm not Dwi-"

Teacher: "Dwight answer can be found in the book!"

Chelsea: "Our teacher is such a peach!"

Eloiza: "You mean she's nice and sweet?"

Chelsea: "No, she has a heart of stone!"

What vegetables do librarians love?

Peas n' quiet!

How do bees go to their school?

They ride the school buzz!

What is a snake's favorite subject?

Hiss-tory!

What does 2+2=5 have in common with your left hand?

It's not right!

Why did the cross-eyed teacher quit?

He couldn't control his pupils!

What do you call a boy who has a dictionary in his pocket?

Smarty Pants!

"Order, class! Order!" the teacher said. What did one student say?

"I'll have some fries and a burger, please."

Why did the new girl come home with a chair from class?

The teacher told her to take a seat!

What did the ghost teacher say to his class?

"Alright, I'll go through it again!"

What are two days in a week that starts with "T"?

Today and Tomorrow!

Is it better to write your homework on an empty stomach or a full stomach?

It's better to write it on a piece of paper!

Why did the pupil eat her homework?

The teacher told them it was a piece of cake!

What turns white when it's dirty and black when it's clean?

A blackboard!

What do you call a bee that can do magic?

A spelling bee!

What's a duck that always gets good grades?

A wise quacker!

What's the capital of Washington?

The letter W!

A teacher went to the cafeteria and ordered soup.

When the cafeteria lady handed over her soup, the teacher said, "Excuse me, I saw your thumb in my soup!"

"Oh it's okay," the cafeteria lady said.

"It wasn't hot."

Teacher: "Where are the students?"

Principal: "Nobel."

Teacher: "Pardon, Sir?"

Principal: "There was Nobel because it's broken! But class was just dismissed!"

Math teacher: "Knock, knock!"

Students: "Who's there?"

Math teacher: "Dozen."

Students: "Dozen who?"

Math teacher: "Dozen anyone want to let me in?"

Percy: "Knock knock!"

Drake: "Who's there?"

Percy: "Europe."

Drake: "Europe who?"

Percy: "Hey! That isn't very nice to say!"

Why did Amy throw the school clock out of the window?

Because she wanted time to fly!

Do pickles enjoy their time at school?

Yes, they relish it!

What is something your teacher will get mad at you for not doing?

Your homework!

How do books keep warm during winter?

They put on their jacket!

What did the bread get detention?

She was loafin' around during class!

Did you learn a lot in school today?

Not enough, I have to go back tomorrow!

PE Teacher: "Knock, knock!"

Students: "Who's there?"

PE Teacher: "Stopwatch."

Students: "Stopwatch who?"

PE Teacher: "Stopwatch you're doing and give me 50 pushups!"

Peter: "Anna, how did you get the answer to the homework?"

Anna: "Alex."

Peter: "Huh?"

Anna: "Alex-plain later!"

Graham: "Mom?"

Mom: "Yes, honey?"

Graham: "Needle."

Mom: "What?"

Graham: "Needle little help with my project!"

Art Teacher: "Knock, knock!"

Students: "Who's there?"

Art Teacher: "Andrew."

Students: "Andrew who?"

Art Teacher: "Andrew a picture! Now it's your turn!"

Librarian: "Quiet, Tina."

Students: "Uhm, none of us are named Tin–"

Librarian: "Quiet Tina library!"

Teacher: "Knock, knock."

Students: "Who's there?"

Teacher: "Major."

Students: "Major who?"

Teacher: "Major day with this joke, haven't I?"

Geography Teacher: "Knock, knock!"

Students: "Who's there?"

Geography Teacher: "Venice."

Students: "Venice who?"

Geography Teacher: "Venice your mother coming home?"

Student: "Teacher, should I use blue or yellow highlighter for the homework?"

Teacher: "Mixed."

Student: "So.. green?"

Teacher: "Mixed no difference. Use whichever!"

Boy: "Knock, knock!"

Girl: "Who's there?"

Boy: "Gerald."

Girl: "Gerald who?"

Boy: "It's Gerald seatmate from last year!"

Student: "Knock, knock!"

Librarian: "Who's there?"

Student: "Noise."

Librarian: "Oh dear, that's not allowed here."

Student: "But it's so noise to be here!"

Dom: "Is our biology teacher sick?"

Addie: "I heard he got a nasty case of bird flu."

Dom: "Man, I knew it! I knew that guy could fly!"

Teacher: "Knock, knock!"

Students: "Who's there?"

Teacher: "Sacha!"

Students: "Sacha who?"

Teacher: "Sacha lot of questions!"

School Bus Driver: "Knock, knock!"

Students: "Who's there?"

School Bus Driver: "Harry."

Students: "Harry who?"

School Bus Driver: "Harry up and get in the bus! It's time to go home!"

Biology Teacher: "Knock, knock!"

Students: "Who's there?"

Biology Teacher: "Ears."

Students: "Ears who?"

Biology Teacher: "Ears another knock knock joke for you!"

In the school clinic...

Nurse: "Oh, another student! What's your name?"

Student: "Lem."

Nurse: "Lem who?"

Student: "Lemme rest please – I've got a headache!"

English Teacher: "Knock, knock!"

Students: "Who's there?"

English Teacher: "Double."

Students: "Double who?"

English Teacher: "W!"

Music Teacher: "Knock, knock!"

Students: "Who's there?"

Music Teacher: "Fiddle."

Students: "Fiddle who?"

Music Teacher: "Fiddle make you happy I'll teacher how to play it!"

Regina: "Knock, knock!"

Cady: "Who's there?"

Regina: "Juana."

Cady: "Juana who?"

Regina: "Juana join me? I'm going to get some cheese fries!"

THE GARDEN

Why can't the weeds fit in the garden anymore?

There wasn't mushroom left!

What in the garden is brown and sticky?
A stick!

How did one flower greet a younger flower?
"Hey, bud!"

What did one bee say to another?
"I love you, honey!"

What tree can you grow in your hand?
A palm tree!

Why was the cabbage's favorite outfit?
The salad dressing!

What happened to the race between the lettuce and the tomato?
The tomato tried to ketchup, but the lettuce was always ahead!

What did the baby corn ask mama corn?
"Where's pop corn?"

Where do mama trees put their baby trees?
In a nursery!

What did the DJ say at the garden party?
"Lettuce turnip the beet, yo!"

Did you hear about the new tree gossip?
I can't be-leaf it!

What's a tree's favorite drink?

Root Beer!

 How do flowers kiss?

They use their tulips!

Gardener: "Knock, knock!"

Flower: "Who's there?"

Gardener: "Seed."

Flower: "Seed who?"

Gardener: "Seed you tomorrow!"

Max went over to see Carl. Carl's nose was big and swollen.

"Whoa, what happened?" Max asked.
"I sniffed a brose," Carl replied.
"Huh?" Max said. "There's no 'b' in rose!"
Carl replied, "There was in this one!"

Potato: "Knock, knock!"

Garlic: "Who's there?"

Potato: "Beets."

Garlic: "Beets who?"

Potato: "Beets me!"

Celery: *follows Lettuce*

Lettuce: "What are you doing?"

Celery: "Stalking you, of course!"

Stringbean 1: "Hey, bro!"

Stringbean 2: "Yo, man!"

Stringbean 1: "Bean a while since we saw each other!"

Gardener: "Knock, knock!"

Terrence: "Who's there?"

Gardener: "Alba."

Terrence: "Alba who?"

Gardener: "Alba in the garden if you need me!"

Bee: "Knock, knock!"

Dragonfly: "Who's there?"

Bee: "Beezer."

Dragonfly: "Beezer who?"

Bee: "Beezer good at making honey!"

Veggie: "Knock, knock!"

Tree: "Who's there?"

Veggie: "Broccoli."

Tree: "Broccoli who?"

Veggie: "Broccoli doesn't have a last name, silly!"

Tulip: "Knock, knock!"

Daisy: "Who's there?"

Tulip: "Henrietta."

Daisy: "Henrietta who?"

Tulip: "Henrietta pear, but it had a worm in it!"

Tomato: "Knock, knock!"

Celery: "Who's there?"

Tomato: "Ketchup."

Celery: "Ketchup who?"

Tomato: "Ketchup with me first, then I'll tell you!"

Dad: "What are you looking for, honey?"

Mom: "I need aggressive fruit!"

Dad: "What? Why?"

Mom: "We need some to make punch!"

Blueberry: "Knock, knock!"

Mango: "Who's there?"

Blueberry: "Berry."

Mango: "Berry who?"

Blueberry: "Berry nice to meet you!"

Tree: "Knock, knock!"

Gardener: "Who's there?"

Tree: "Figs."

Gardener: "Figs who?"

Tree: "Figs the hose, we need water!"

Bee: "Knock, knock!"

Flower: "Who's there?"

Bee: "Honey bee."

Flower: "Honey bee who?"

Bee: "Honey bee a dear and get that for me please!"

Tree: "Knock, knock!"

Bird: "Who's there?"

Tree: "Olive."

Bird: "Olive who?"

Tree: "Olive you!"

What do you say to a fancy cactus?

"Looking sharp, bro!"

What's a flower that always makes up stories?

A lie-lac!

How does the flower ride its bike?

Using its petals!

What is the saddest tree in the garden?

A weeping willow!

How do you know when a tree is addicted to the Internet?

They're always logged in!

What plant likes to roar in the garden?

A dandelion!

How did the potato become a good detective?

He keeps his eyes peeled.

What is an insect's favorite band?

The Beetles!

What do you get when two spiders marry?

Newly webs!

Gardener: "Knock, knock!"

Butler: "Who's there?"

Gardener: "Mango!"

Butler: "Mango who?"

Gardener: "Mango to the door and just open it!"

Abby: "Knock, knock!"

Julie: "Who's there?"

Abby: "Abby."

Julie: "Abby who?"

Abby: "Abby just stung me!"

Parrot: "What are you doing?"

Pirate: "Garden."

Parrot: "What?"

Pirate: "Garden the treasure, it's precious!"

Bee: "Knock, knock!"

Monkey: "Who's there?"

Bee: "Comb."

Monkey: "Comb who?"

Bee: "Comb on down and I'll tell you!"

Flower: "Knock, knock!"

Beetle: "Who's there?"

Flower: "Daisy."

Beetle: "Daisy who?"

Flower: "Daisy me rollin', they hatin'!"

Mama grass: "Knock knock!"

Baby grass: "Who's there?"

Mama grass: "Mom sprout."

Baby grass: "Mom sprout who?"

Mama grass: "Mom sprout of you! You've grown so much!"

Orange: "Knock, knock!"

Lemon: "Who's there?"

Orange: "Orange."

Lemon: "Orange who?"

Orange: "Orange you sick of all these knock-knock jokes?"

Sun: "Knock, knock!"

Tree: "Who's there?"

Sun: "Ray."

Tree: "Ray who?"

Sun: "You don't Ray-member me?!"

Strawberry: "Knock, knock!"

Kiwi: "Who's there?"

Strawberry: "Jam."

Kiwi: "Jam who?"

Strawberry: "Jam mind helping me out of this jar?"

Mom: "Can you see anything outside?"

Dad: "Snow."

Mom: "But it's summer?"

Dad: "I meant there's Snow-body there!"

Gardener: "Knock, knock!"

Arianne: "Who's there?"

Gardener: "Hand."

Arianne: "Hand who?"

Gardener: "Handover the shovel please!"

Ana: "Knock, knock!"

Evand: "Who's There?"

Ana: "Banana."

Evand: "Banana who?"

Ana: "Knock, knock!"

Evand: "Who's There?"

Ana: "Banana."

Evand: "Banana who?"

Ana: "Knock, knock!"

Evand: "Who's There?"

Ana: "Orange."

Evand: "Orange who?"

Ana: "Orange you glad it's not banana again?"

Farmer: "Wanna know to get that beautiful country girl's attention?"

Gardener: "How?"

Farmer: "A tractor!"

Monkey: "You know why jokes about tree branches so good?"

Squirrel: "Why?"

Monkey: "Because they have so many levels to them!"

How can you tell it's a dogwood tree?

By the bark!

Why did the worm cross the ruler?

He wanted to become an inch worm!

What cake is popular among the birds?

Chocolate chirp!

What is the shortest month of the year?

May-- it only has three letters!

What season is it best to play on a trampoline?

During spring time!

What rabbit has lots of fleas?

Bugs Bunny!

What do you call a baker's garden?

A "flour" garden!

What's a daisy with three eyes?

A daiiisy!

Where did the caterpillars go to pray?

In a ch-apple!

A STROLL AROUND TOWN

Why can't the hyena cross the road?

He's too busy laughing!

What did the traffic light say to the car?

"Stop looking, I'm still changing!"

What's a fly with no wings?

A walk!

How did the trash collector get good at his job?

He just picked it up as he went along!

What did one baseball cap say to the other?

"Bye, I'm going on ahead."

How can you tell that the duck didn't pay for the lip stick?

She has it on her bill!

What is the frog's favorite meal at McDonald's?

French flies with Diet Croak.

What did the Dalmatian say after eating at the diner?

"That sure hit the spot!"

Why didn't the koala bear become a teacher?

She was over-koala-fied for the job!

What did the volcano say as the birds passed him by?

"I lava all of you!"

What did the apple say to the fruit vendor?

Nothing. Apples can't talk.

Why can't the cheese chase the macaroni?

Because it's a lot pasta than him!

Why was the clock asked to leave the library?

Because it tocks too much.

When are most twins born in the hospital?

During twos-days!

What did the reporter ask the ice cream man?

"So what's the scoop?"

What on the street has four wheels and flies?

A garbage truck!

How does the paint store answer their phone?

"Yellow there!"

Old man: "Knock, knock!"

Waitress: "Who's there?"

Old man: "Theresa."

Waitress: "Theresa who?"

Old man: "Theresa fly in my soup."

Clown: "Knock, knock!"

Karen: "Who's there?"

Clown: "Abby."

Karen: "Abby who?"

Clown: "Abby birthday to you!"

Baker: "Knock, knock."

Suzie: "Who's there?"

Baker: "Muffin."

Suzie: "Muffin who?"

Baker: "Muffin the matter with me, how about you?"

Driver: "Knock, Knock!"

Arnold: "Who's there?"

Driver: "Cargo!"

Arnold: "Cargo who?"

Driver: "Car go beep, beep!"

A guy is staying at home when someone knocks at the door. He answers it and sees a snail staring up at him. He picks it up and throws it as far as he can. A year later, someone knocks again. The guy opens it and sees the same snail. The snail looks mad.

"What was that all about?"

Justin: "Knock! Knock!"

Selena: "Who's there?"

Justin: "Justin."

Selena: "Justin who?"

Justin: "Justin the neighborhood and thought I'd see you."

Baker: "Knock, knock!"

Kevin: "Who's there?"

Baker: "Icing."

Kevin: "Icing who?"

Baker: "Icing so loudly everyone can hear me!"

Candyman: "Knock, knock!"

Willie: "Who's there?"

Candyman: "Imogen."

Willie: "Imogen who?"

Candyman: "Imogen life without sweets!"

Oswald: "Knock, knock!"

Ed: "Who's there?"

Oswald: "Oswald."

Ed: "Oswald who?"

Oswald: "Oswald my chewing gum by mistake!"

Tony: "Knock, knock!"

Gringo: "Who's there?"

Tony: "Pasta."

Gringo: "Pasta who?"

Tony: "Pasta la vista, Gringo!"

What time do people start throwing pieces of bread at your head?

Time to duck!

Why did the police arrest the chef?

Because she got caught beating some eggs!

Why does that banana get all the girls swooning for him?

Because he's a banana smoothie!

Pizza man: "Knock, knock!"

Doug: "Who's there?"

Pizza man: "18D."

Doug: "18D who?"

Pizza man: "18D whole pizza! I'm sorry!"

Customer: "Excuse me, there is a fly in my soup."

Waitress: "Oh it's okay, Sir. The spider in your bread will catch it."

Why are scissors always early?

They always take shortcuts!

Why was the pigeon in the ambulance?

Because it needed some tweetment!

Where does the T-rex buy her clothes?

The dino-store!

What did the egg do when it was getting dark?

He scrambled home!

What falls on the street but never gets hurt?

Snow!

Why did the baker put the candles on top of the birthday cake?

Because he can't light them from the bottom!

Where do kittens like to go for their field trip?

To the mew-seum!

What key can't open any doors?

A turkey!

How did the chewing gum cross the road?

It was stuck on an elephant's foot!

There was once an old couple who went to a restaurant and ordered two burgers. The waiter brought the burgers and the old man started to eat. The waiter noticed that the woman was only staring at the food. He went to ask them if there was a problem. The old woman said nothing and just stared at him, but the old man smiled and said, "Oh, the sandwich is delicious! But she can't eat yet because I am still using her teeth!"

Mom: "Eat your roast chicken, son. It's got iron it!"

Jim: "So that's why it's so tough!"

A mushroom walks into a bar. Everyone immediately went to talk to him. Who could blame them, though? He looks like such a fungi!

Bob: "Why don't we TACO 'bout it?"

Josie: "No! It's over! I'm NACHO girlfriend anymore!"

Whenever I say that I'll start eating healthy, a chocolate bar stares at me and Snickers.

Nana: "Knock, knock."

Helga: "Who's there?"

Nana: "A little old lady."

Helga: "A little old lady who?"

Nana: "Wow, I didn't know you could yodel!"

Tailor: "Knock, knock!"

Laila: "Who's there?"

Tailor: "Euripides."

Laila: "Euripides who?"

Tailor: "If Euripides dress, you need to pay for them!"

Noah: "Knock knock!"

Sean: "Who's there?"

Noah: "Police."

Sean: "Why, Officer? Did I do anything wrong?"

Noah: "No, I meant POLICE let me in, it's so cold out here!"

Barber: "Knock knock!"

Gabe: "Who's there?"

Barber: "Mustache."

Gabe: "Mustache who?"

Barber: "I mustache you a question!"

Mayor: "Knock, knock!"

Nicole: "Who's there?"

Mayor: "Avenue."

Nicole: "Avenue who?"

Mayor: "Avenue met me before? My dear, nice to meet you!"

Rey: "Will you remember me in a minute?"

Ben: "Yes."

Rey: "Will you remember me in a day?"

Ben: "Yes."

Rey: "Knock, knock."

Ben: "Who's there?"

Rey: "I thought you would remember me!"

Angelica: "Knock, knock!"

Tommy: "Who's there?"

Angelica: "Iona."

Tommy: "Iona who?"

Angelica: "Iona new toy!"

Shoemaker: "Knock, knock!"

Chuck: "Who's there?"

Shoemaker: "Amish."

Chuck: "Amish who?"

Shoemaker: "My goodness, lad. You're not a shoe!

Locksmith: "Knock, knock!"

Hans: "Who's there?"

Locksmith: "Lock."

Hans: "Lock who?"

Locksmith: "Lock who it is, after all this time!"

Loretta: "Can you tell me your friend's secret?"

Melanie: "Nonna."

Loretta: "What?"

Melanie: "Nonna your business! Gossip's bad!"

Why did the police arrest the chicken?

Because there might be fowl play!

Why did the garden shrub go to the barber?

It needed a trim!

What do firemen like to eat with their soup?

Firecrackers!

Why didn't skeletons get into street fights?

They don't have the guts!

What can you always see at the end of every road?

The letter "D".

PLAYTIME

Why did the children cross the playground?

To check out the other SLIDE!

What animal can you always find at baseball games?

A bat!

What did the rabbit say when she lost a Wii game?

"Hey, I want a Wii-match!"

Why is Cinderella bad at soccer?

She always runs away from the ball!

Why do you need to bring two pairs of pants when playing golf?

In case you get a hole in one!

What's a squid's favorite game?

Arm wrestling!

When do basketball players need to go to the doctor?

When they get a hooping cough!

Why did the frog love baseball?

He's a pro at catching a fly!

Why isn't it fun to play hockey with pigs?

They tend to hog the puck!

Why did the baker join the baseball team?

They needed a batter!

How do porcupines win every game?

They always have the most points!

What is the most popular sport among insects?

Cricket!

Les: "Knock, knock!"

Alex: "Who's there?"

Les: "Les!"

Alex: "Les who?"

Les: "Les go out and play tag!"

Vicky: "What's your favorite game?"

Haden: "Haden."

Vicky: "What?"

Haden: "Haden Seek!"

Rabbit: "Knock, knock!"

Turtle: "Who's there?"

Rabbit: "Foster!"

Turtle: "Foster who?"

Rabbit: "Foster! They might catch you!"

Mom: "Honey, I heard you got hurt while playing! What happened?"

Hannah: "Mom! Many!"

Mom: "Many?"

Hannah: "The left one! I scraped MANY, Mom!"

Bruce: "Knock, knock!"

Alfred: "Who's there?"

Bruce: "Bruce."

Alfred: "Bruce who?"

Bruce: "I Bruce easily! I should be careful while playing."

Mario: "Knock, knock!"

Luigi: "Who's there?"

Mario: "Lego."

Luigi: "Lego who?"

Mario: "Lego of me and I'll tell you!"

Vanessa: "Knock, knock!"

Troy: "Who's there?"

Vanessa: "Tennis."

Troy: "Tennis who?"

Vanessa: "Tennis is five plus five!"

Ethel: "Knock, knock!"

Dara: "Who's there?"

Ethel: "Hockey."

Dara: "Hockey who?"

Ethel: "Hockey doesn't work, so I had to knock!"

Oh no! Diego fell down the well while playing tag!

I knew he couldn't see that well!

Brad: "Hey! Where's coach?"

Ethan: "He's at the bank."

Brad: "Why?"

Ethan: "He needs his quarterback."

It's sad to ask your friends out to play on a Sunday, but the day before would be a sadder day!

Skeleton: "Can I play soccer with you guys?"

Dylan: "Sorry, man. It's going to take some guts!"

Team Captain 1: "We want a rematch!"

Team Captain 2: "You don't need the perfect match! Just use a lighter."

Dylan signed up for a marathon, but he's not quite sure if it's the real deal or just a run through.

Lilo: "Nani! Stitch and I decided to take up fencing."

Nani: "That sounds fun, Lilo!"

Lilo: "But the neighbors keep telling us that we should put it back!"

What's the hardest thing to catch while playing tag?

Your breath!

What snack do basketball players love?

Donuts-- because they can dunk them!

What runs all around a recess field but never moves?

The school fence!

What position in soccer do ghosts love best?

Ghoul keeper!

Why are waiters so good at tennis?

Because they can serve well!

Why are football players always so cool?

They sit close to their fans!

Why do pitchers raise one leg when throwing the ball?

If they raise both legs, they'd fall down!

What did the baseball glove tell the ball before the game?

"Catch ya later, dude!"

What's black and white and spins round and round?

A penguin tumbling down after tug-of-war!

No one could predict what that camera's next moves in the field would be! What a loose Canon!

Coach: "Hey, it's almost time for your race! Have you eaten?"

Sprinters: "No, coach. We FASTed!"

Two photos wanted to try out boxing, so the coach weighed them both using Instagrams!

What's sport loves its country most?

Flag football!

Howard: "Knock, knock!"

Bernadette: "Who's there?"

Howard: "Howard."

Bernadette: "Howard who?"

Howard: "Howard you like to play dodgeball with us?"

Team Captain: "Coach! What do we need to win the next basketball match?"

Coach: "Amanda."

Team Captain: "Amanda who?"

Coach: "Amanda can coach you like me! I'll make you win!"

Terry: "Who's chasing Peter just now?"

Amy: "Doug."

Terry: "Doug who?"

Amy: "I meant he was being chased by a Doug!"

During Trust Falls...

Lemon: "Okay, here I go!"

Apple: "Oh no! A lemon drop!"

Team Captain: "Why can't our hands be 12 inches long?"

Coach: "Because then it would be a foot!"

Boomerang: "Time out! I need to go to the bathroom!"

Stick: "Okay. Will you be coming back?"

Boomerang: "I always do!"

How do you deal with a fear of tripping over speed bumps?

Don't worry, you'll slowly get over it.

How can mummies win during games?

They have to urn it!

Weightlifter 1: "What is heavy forward but not backward?"

Weightlifter 2: "What?"

Weightlifter 1: "A ton."

I feel bad for the fridge magnet while playing Hide n' Seek. It's got ten fridges running after it now!

Why was the burglar so mad when they didn't win at soccer?

Because he takes things personally!

Why did the girl go up the ladder during Hide-and-Seek?
She wanted to get the upper hand!

What happened when the clock lost during tag?

He was ticked off!

What's Tarzan's favorite spot in the playground?
The swing, of course!

How did the bird find the elephant hiding in the fridge?
The door won't shut!

What in the playground can you catch but not throw?
A cold!

Why did the net love volleyball so much?
He can always be outstanding in the field!

What game do pirates hate?

The Boat Is Sinking!

What do you call a dinosaur that is tired after running all day?

A dino-SORE!

Why didn't the skeleton try the see-saw?

He had no body to try it with.

What is the hardest part in going down the slide?

The ground!

OUTER SPACE

What did the astronaut do when he saw a green alien?

He waited until it was ripe!

Why do astronauts smell so nice?

Because they love taking meteor showers!

What can you find at the center of Jupiter?

The letter "I."

How do galaxies throw the perfect space party?

They planet!

Why can't the spaceship park on the moon?

She's full already.

Why does Mickey Mouse go to space everyday?

He needs to feed Pluto!

How do you help an astronaut's baby fall asleep?

You rock-et!

What happened when the astronaut hit his head?

He kept seeing stars!

What medicine do aliens take for headaches?

Space capsules.

What do you call a star with sunglasses?

A movie star!

Why do aliens love computer keyboards?

Because they have space bars!

Where do planets eat their dinner?

On flying saucers!

What do stars like to read?

Comet books!

Why was Venus jealous of Saturn?

She wanted a ring, too!

Who did the squirrel look for in space?

The astro-nut!

When do astronauts like eat lunch?

At LAUNCH time!

What do aliens like to listen to?

Nep-tunes!

What happens to the sun when it reads books?

It gets brighter!

Alien: "Knock, knock!"

Astronaut: "Who's there?"

Alien: "Pizza."

Astronaut: "Pizza who?"

Alien: "We come in Pizza!"

Alien: "Knock, knock!"

Astronaut: "Who's there?"

Alien: "Alien."

Astronaut: "Alien who?"

Alien: "Uhhm. Do you have many alien friends?"

Astronaut 1: "See that?"

Astronaut 2: "What?"

Astronaut 1: "Kenya!"

Astronaut 2: "Where?"

Astronaut 1: "Kenya see it now?"

Astronaut 1: "See that?"

Astronaut 2: "What?"

Astronaut 1: "Jamaica!"

Astronaut 2: "Do you mean... that?"

Astronaut 1: "Jamaica mistake. It's there!"

Astronaut 1: "See that?"

Astronaut 2: "What?"

Astronaut 1: "Utah!"

Astronaut 2: "Where?"

Astronaut 1: "Bro, Utah one who pointed it out to me awhile ago!"

Astronaut 1: "Wow, Europe!"

Astronaut 2: "What?"

Astronaut 1: "Europe early this morning! Time to explore space again!"

Alien: "Knock, knock!"

Astronaut: "Who's there?"

Alien: "Al."

Astronaut: "Al who?"

Alien: "Al attack your rocket if you don't let me in!"

Astronaut 1: "What did Tennessee?"

Astronaut 2: "What?"

Astronaut 1: "The same thing as Arkansas!"

Astronaut 1: "Whoa! Look at how detailed that ocean is!"

Astronaut 2: "Of course! It's the Pacific!"

Astronaut 1: "Which state has the most streets?"

Astronaut 2: "What?"

Astronaut 1: "Rhode Island!"

Astronaut 1: "I don't like the Orion's belt!"

Astronaut 2: "Why not?"

Astronaut 1: "I think it's a waist of space!"

Astronaut 1: "I have a few jokes about retired astronauts."

Astronaut 2: "Let me hear 'em!"

Astronaut 1: "Nah, none of them work."

Alien mom: "Our son put his shoes on the wrong feet!"

Alien dad: "I know! I don't even know where he got someone else's feet!"

Alien: "Tell us, humans! What's the most ground-breaking invention on earth today?"

Astronaut: "A shovel!"

Alien 1: "Put the spaceship on reverse! You'll feel nostalgic."

Alien 2: "How?"

Alien 1: "It'll take you back, I promise!"

Astronaut 1: "Claustrophobia?"

Astronaut 2: "Yeah."

Astronaut 1: "It's okay, you just really need to think outside the box."

Alien: "Human! What do you call a three-footed aardvark?"

Astronaut: "A yardvark!"

Three astronauts walk into a space bar.

Wow, those are some tiny astronauts!

Alien: "What do you humans means by a rhetorical question?"

How did the hipster astronaut burn his tongue?

He drank his morning coffee it was cool.

Alien: "Can you drop an egg on a concrete floor without cracking it?"

Astronaut: "Here in space? No, it will just float!"

Astronaut 1: "We can lift an elephant with one hand here!"

Astronaut 2: "No. Elephants only have feet!"

How do you make an alien egg roll?

Just give it a little push.

Alien 1: "What can we get if we conquer Switzerland?"

Alien 2: "Well, their flag is a big plus!"

Alien: "We found a monster on earth! It has one horn and gives milk!"

Astronaut: "Uhhmm. A milk truck?"

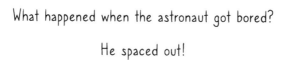

Why did the cow want to go to space?

She wanted to see the MOOOOOOn!

After landing, what did the alien say to the grass?

"Take me to your weeder!"

What happened when the astronaut got bored?

He spaced out!

What disease can aliens get in space?

Missles!

Why isn't there any air in space?

The Milky Way would go bad!

Why did the rocket ship need to go to the doctor?

He needed to get booster shots!

What do you do when you find a spaceman?

Park in it, man!

What school do planets and stars go to?

The UNIVERSity!

What in space is fast, loud, and tasty?

A rocket chip!

Why did the alien ask for more beef on his pizza?

He liked them meteor!

Which Star Wars droid takes the longest route?

R2 Detour!

How do we help hold the moon up?

Using moon beams!

Alien: "Knock, knock!"

Astronaut: "Who's there?"

Alien: "Pizza."

Astronaut: "Pizza who?"

Alien: "We come in Pizza!"

How much money does the moon have?

One dollar-- it has four quarters!

A BEACH PARTY

How does the ocean say hi to her friends?

She waves at them!

How did the sand greet the tides when they came in?
"Long tide, no sea!"

What do trees wear to beach parties?
Their swimming trunks!

Why didn't fish take vacations that much?
Because they live in schools!

Why didn't the whale like eating clownfish?

They tasted too funny.

What's a foot long, slippery, and floats on water?
A slipper.

How do you make an octopus laugh?
Use ten-tickles!

Who's the best underwater secret agent of all time?
Pond. James Pond.

Why do squids live in saltwater?
Pepper water would make them sneeze!

What's the same between turtles and beaches?
They have shells!

Why did the banana put on sunscreen before going to the beach?
She didn't want to peel!

Why did the puffer fish blush?
Because the sea weed!

What on the beach is tasty and can do magic?
The sand-witch!

What's the sailor's least favorite vegatable?
Leeks!

Barbie: "Knock, knock!"
Ken: "Who's there?"
Barbie: "Barbie."
Ken: "Barbie who?"
Barbie: "Barbie-qued chicken is ready for the beach party!"

Giant: "Wow, the beach!"
Jack: "It's BEAN a while since we last went here!"

Noah: "Knock, knock!"
Emma: "Who's there?"
Noah: "Noah."
Emma: "Noah who?"
Noah: "Noah good place we could build a sandcastle?"

Boat: "Knock, knock!"

Paddle: "Who's there?"

Boat: "Yacht."

Paddle: "Yacht who?"

Boat: "Yacht a know me by now!"

Fish: "Knock, knock!"
Pirate: "Who's there?"
Fish: "Urchin."
Pirate: "Urchin who?"
Fish: "Urchin looks really pointy!"

Lilo: "Knock, knock!"
Stitch: "Who's there?"
Lilo: "Hawaii."
Stitch: "Hawaii who?"
Lilo: "I'm good. Hawaii you?"

Crocodile: "Knock knock!"

Turtle: "Who's there?"

Crocodile: "Canoe."

Turtle: "Canoe who?"
Crocodile: "Canoe come out of your shell now? It's fun out here!"

Katara: "Knock, knock!"
Sokka: "Who's there?"
Katara: "Water."
Sokka: "Water who?"
Katara: "Water way to enjoy the day!"

Bill: "Knock, knock!"
Steve: "Who's there?"
Bill: "Yah!"
Steve: "Yah who?"
Bill: "I'm glad you're enjoying this beach party!"

Sheep: "Knock, knock!"
Fox: "Who's there?"
Sheep: "Barbara."
Fox: "Barbara who?"
Sheep: "Barbara black sheep, have you any wool..."

Fisherman: "Knock, knock!"

Lifeguard: "Who's there?"

Fisherman: "Hey."

Lifeguard: "Hey who?"

Fisherman: "Hey ho, hey ho, it's off to work we go!"

DJ: "Knock, knock!"

Party host: "Who's there?"

DJ: "Radio."

Party host: "Radio who?"

DJ: "Radio not, here I come!"

Fruit: "Knock, knock!"

Veggies: "Who's there?"

Fruit: "Passion."

Veggies: "Passion who?"

Fruit: "Just Passion by for the party!"

Penguin: "Knock, knock!"

Elephant: "Who's there?"

Penguin: "Icy."

Elephant: "Icy who?"

Penguin: "Can't you see me? Do you need new glasses?"

What is the best day to go to the beach?
SUN-day!

Why did the police show up at the ocean?
Something seemed fishy!

What do you call seagulls that fly near the bay?
Bagels.

What is the heaviest part of the fish?
His scales!

Why is ice cream always invited during beach parties?
Because he's so cool!

What do you get when you throw a yellow sun hat in the water?
A wet yellow sun hat!

Why did the teacher jump into the sea?
She needed to test the water first!

What's a crayfish who wouldn't clean his room?
A slobster!

What's the favorite snack of sea monsters?
Fish and ships!

How did the tide pool greet the other tide pool?
"C'mon man, show off those mussels!"

Why did the seaweed close its eyes?
It can see the ocean's bottom!

Why are fish careful when eating worms?
They might get hooked on them!

What waves can you find in small beaches?
Microwaves!

What does Cinderella wear when she swims?
Glass flippers!

Why did the burglar hide in the beach showers?
He wanted to come clean!

What did the seaweed say when it got stuck under a rock?
"KELP! KELP!"

Look! All 26 letters went out for a swim!
How AlphaWETical!

Singing in the beach showers is fun until you get soap in your mouth.
Then it's going to be a SOAP opera!

Jim: "Knock, knock."
Eli: "Who's there?"
Jim: "Jim."
Eli: "Jim who?"
Jim: "Jim mind if I join you?"

Mom: "Honey, please don't go to the waters naked!"
Girl: "I'm not naked, Mom! I'm wearing sunscreen!"

Dad: "Look at my new shirt, son!"
Son: "Dad, are you going to be handsome, or are you going to wear
THAT?"

What's the difference between a red apple and a green apple?
The red apple got too much sun at the beach!

Anyone who needs an ark?
I Noah guy!

A doctor went for a deep dive and saw a dolphin under the sea.

Dolphin: "Hello! Nice to meet you! What's your name?"
Doctor: "Bublluuuuubbblluubbb-"

Watermelon: "Look, that velcro's selling souvenirs!"
Banana: "Oh, I wouldn't buy anything from velcro. He's a total rip-off."

Cliff: "I can't believe I got fired from the calendar factory!"
Rick: "Why, what happened?"
Cliff. "All I did was take a day off!"

Elephant: "You should always buy swimming trunks with holes in them."
Monkey: "Why?"
Elephant: "It's the only way to get your feet in!"

Scuba Diver 1: "Why do we always fall backwards into the water?"
Scuba Diver 2: "Well if we fell forward, we'd still end up in the boat!"

Did you hear the joke about the beach umbrella?
Forget it, it'll go over your head.

Why is it hard to stay friends with trees?
They can be a little shady!

Why did the letter "R" get mad at the pirate?
Because he said his first love will always be the "C"!

What did the sardines say about about the submarine?
"Look! A can of people!"

Where do you need to take a sick boat?
To the dock!

TIME FOR BED

What do you call a sleeping pizza?

A piZZZZZZZZa!

What can't the Gingerbread Man sleep without?
His cookie sheet!

What do scuba divers need to wear in bed?
Snore-kels!

What can make baby sharks sleepy?
Bite-time stories!

Why don't teddy bears ask for midnight snacks?
They're stuffed already!

Why does a bed grow longer at night?
Because it gets two feet added to it!

Where do mermaids love to sleep?
A waterbed.

What do you get if you put candy under your pillow?
Sweet dreams!

Why did the bicycle fall to the ground?
Because he's two-tired!

What should you do if you find a tiger sleeping in your bed?
Run and find another bed to sleep in!

Where do sunflowers sleep at night?
In their flowerbed!

How do spies sleep?
They go undercover!

Where do toilets nap?
In the restroom!

Mom: "Knock, knock!"
Julia: "Who's there?"
Mom: "Lenny!"
Julia: "Lenny who?"
Mom: "Lenny tuck you to bed, sweetie. It's time for bed!"

Window: "Knock, knock."
Dina: "Who's there?"
Window: "House."
Dina: "House who?"
Window: "House your day today? Was it fun?"

Earl: "Knock, knock!"

Alarm clock: "Who's there?"

Earl: "Earl."

Alarm clock: "Earl who?"

Earl: "Earl be excited to get to bed! I'm so tired."

Blanket: "Knock, knock!"

Pillow: "Who's there?"

Blanket: "Bed."

Pillow: "Bed who?"

Blanket: "Bed you can't guess who I am!"

If James refuses to go to bed, is he guilty of resisting a rest?

Mom: "I'll fix you a nice cup of hot cocoa!"

Kettle: *whispers to the boiling water* "I'm sorry, guys. You will be mist!"

Dog: "Look! You have a head and four legs, too!"

Bed: "Yeah. I also have a foot!"

Dog: *wags tail happily*

Mom: "Sleeping with a sore throat again?"

Dad: "Yeah. They're such a pain in the neck!"

What does a house like to wear in bed?

Address!

Dad: "I love telling Dad jokes!"
Mom: "Yeah, sometimes he even laughs!"

How do you find out which direction the sun will rise when you wake up?
It will dawn on you eventually.

Why do mountains have the funniest bedtime stories?

They're just so hill-areas!

Jaimie: "Dad, when does a dad joke cost $1000?"
Dad: "When it's a granddad joke!"

What do buildings do after tucking their baby buildings to sleep?
They choose one of their stories to tell!

Dave: "What's the best time to wake up?"
Alarm clock: "6:30am, hands down!"

Why did the little girl run around her bed?
To catch up on her sleep!

How do you know if an elephant is hiding under your bed?
When your bed reaches the ceiling!

What do you call a sleepy bull?
A bulldozer!

How do you know when you're good at sleeping?
You can do it with your eyes closed!

What do you call a woodcutter who loves to sleep?
A slumberjack!

Why can't the baby monster go to sleep?
He had a nightmare about humans!

Why did the snake sleep in a hotel?
To get suite-dreams!

How did the musician sleep last night?
He slept soundly!

What did the mama cow say to the baby cow?
"Honey, it's pasture bedtime!"

What do fruits tell each other at bedtime?
Berry tales!

How do you let a tree sleep at night?
You leaf it alone.

What does Batgirl wear whenever she sleeps?
Her Dark Knight gown!

What did the cook give her baby while tucking her to bed?
A chef's kiss!

English Teacher: "Where's the 25th letter of the alphabet? It's time to sleep!"
The letter "A": "I don't know. Y?"

Carla: "I saw a thesaurus today!"
Mom: "Wow! Tell me about it!"
Carla: "That dinosaur knew so many big words!"

Butterfly: "Ssshhh, the bee is already sleeping."
Bee: "No! Thizzz izzz juzzz how I zzzzound!"

Dad: "Why did you sell our vacuum?"
Mom: "It's just collecting dust now!"

What do vegan zombies like to snack on during midnights?
"GRAAAAAAAIIIIIINS!!!"

Johnny: "Can I borrow your bookmark?"
Toby: "My name's Toby, not Mark!"

Three conspiracy theorists went to bed at 9PM.
That's definitely not just a coincidence!

Mama sheep: "How many of my baby sheep are still awake?"
Shepherd: "Let's see. One, two, zzzzzzz-"

We wanted to watch The Neverending Story last night, but we couldn't finish it!

What did Dad say to the bedroom wall?
"One more crack like that and I'll have to plaster you!"

Why did the cookie dough fall asleep?
The baker let it rest!

What did the mama goat say to her kid?
"GOAT-to sleep!"

What did the pillowcase say to the pillow?
"Don't worry, I've got you covered!"

Where do fish go to sleep?
On the seabed!

Why do dragons sleep during the day?
So they can be ready to fight knights!

Have you heard the elephant's joke about his bed?
He hasn't made it yet!

DREAMLAND

What do you call a dream about an orange sea?

A Fanta-sea!

How can you get yourself to dream about magical forests?
Simple! Sleep like a log!

What do you call an elf with lots of money?
Welfy!

What gift did the mermaid want for her birthday?
A shell phone to call her friends!

Why did the girl go back to bed?
To follow her dreams!

What do knights look for when they are scared of the dark?
Their knight light!

How many sorcerers do you need to change a light bulb?
Depends on what you want to change it into!

What do elves first learn in school?
The elf-abet!

What happens when a bee has a spell on him?
He is bee-witched!

How did Jack find out how many beans his cow was worth?
Using a cow-culator!

What do you call a fairy hates taking showers?
Stinkerbell!

What subject do they teach at wizard school?
Spelling!

What songs did the Mummy listen to?
Wrap music.

Three friends got stranded on a deserted island. One day, they find a magic lamp. Inside is a genie who tells them he'd grant each friend one wish.

Friend 1: "I want to go home!"
Her wish was granted.

Friend 2: "I want to go home, too!"
And the genie also granted her wish.

Friend 3: "I'm lonely. I wish my friends were back here with me!"

Pirate: "Knock, knock!"
Parrot: "Who's there?"
Pirate: "Clumsy pirate."
Parrot: "Clumsy pi-"
Pirate: "ARRRRRRR I FELL INTO THE WATER AAARRRGGGHH!"

Witch: "Knock, knock!"
Wizard: "Who's there?"
Witch: "Spell."
Wizard: "Spell who?"
Witch: "W-H-O!"

Ghost: "Knock, knock!"
Frankenstein: "Who's there?"
Ghost: "Boo!"
Frankenstein: "Boo who?"
Ghost: "Oh, it was just a joke! Please don't cry!"

Mummy: "Knock, knock!"
Zombie: "Who's there?"
Mummy: "King Tut."
Zombie: "King Tut who?"
Mummy: "King Tut-key fried chicken!"

Wizard: "Wow! What a beautiful owl! Let's try talking to it!"
Owl: "Hoo?"
Wizard: "Hoo!"
Owl: "Hooooo!"
Wizard: "Hoo hoo!"
Owl: "Oh, I'm sorry! I didn't mean it that way."

What do vampires stay away from when dining in a cafe?
A STAKE sandwich!

What do you call a mean ghost?
A BOO-lly!

Witch: "Knock, knock!"
Wizard: "Who's there?"
Witch: "Voodoo."
Wizard: "Voodoo who?"
Witch: "Voodoo you think it is? It's me, your old friend!"

Fairy: "Have you heard of the big, friendly giant?"
Dwarf: "Of course! I look up to the guy!"

Ghost: "Knock, knock!"
Zombie: "Who's there?"
Ghost: "Ivor."
Zombie: "Ivor who?"
Ghost: "Ivor you let me in or I'll simply pass through the door!"

Unicorn: "Knock, knock!"
Snail: "Who's there?"
Unicorn: "Abbot."
Snail: "Abbot who?"
Unicorn: "Abbot you can't catch me!"

Knight 1: "Knock, knock!"

Knight 2: "Who's there?"

Knight 1: "Armageddon."

Knight 2: "Armageddon who?"

Knight 1: "Armageddon a little bored! Can we do something fun?"

Frankenstein: "Knock, knock!"

Banshee: "Who's there?"

Frankenstein: "Shocking."

Banshee: "Shocking who?"

Frankenstein: "Shocking you!"

Pinocchio: "Knock, knock!"

Geppetto: "Who's there?"

Pinocchio: "Wooden shoe."

Geppetto: "Wooden shoe who?"

Pinocchio: "Wooden shoe like to hear another joke?"

What did the mermaid say when the fishes wouldn't eat their food?
Water you waiting for?

What did the bald eagle dream about?
Having beautiful hair!

What's the Frog Prince's favorite year?
The leap year!

What fish did the pirate get for a pet?
A swordfish!

What vampire won't stop eating?
Snack-ula!

What makes leprechauns great with plants?
They have green fingers!

How should you talk to giants?
You should use BIG words!

What's a pirate's favorite subject in school?
AAAAARRRRT!!!

Who did the zombie take on a date?
His ghoul-friend!

How do vampires get sick?
They start coffin hard!

Who is big, green and loves to play a lot of tricks?
Prank-enstein!

What did the tooth fairy need to fix her wand?
Some toothpaste!

How did the dwarf greet the flowers?
"How's it growin'?"

What haircut did the fairy get?
A pixie cut!

FBI Agent: "Knock, knock!"
Spy: "Who's there?"
FBI Agent: "Keanu."
Spy: "Keanu who?"
FBI Agent: "Keanu let me in? I just have a few questions!"

Rey: "Knock, knock!"
Ben: "Who's there?"
Rey: "Obi Wan."
Ben: "Obi Wan who?"
Rey: "Obi Wan of the good guys!"

Princess: "Knock, knock!"
Becky: "Who's there?"
Princess: "Sarah."
Becky: "Sarah who?"
Princess: "Sa-rah phone I could use there?"

Becky: "Knock, knock!"

Sarah: "Who's there?"

Becky: "Phone."

Sarah: "Phone who?"

Becky: "Phonely I'd known it was you!"

Tooth Fairy: "Knock, knock!"

Dentist: "Who's there?"

Tooth Fairy: "Tooth."

Dentist: "Tooth who?"

Tooth Fairy: "Why yes, I love wearing those!"

T-Rex: "Knock, knock!"

Pterodactyl: "Who's there?"

T-Rex: "Fossil."

Pterodactyl: "Fossil who?"

T-Rex: "Fossil last time, please open the door!"

Joker: "Knock, knock!"

Prince: "Who's there?"

Joker: "Jester."

Prince: "Jester who?"

Joker: "Jester silly old man! Ha ha!"

Troy: "Knock, knock!"

Gabriella: "Who's there?"

Troy: "Troy."

Gabriella: "Troy who?"

Troy: "Troy out for the musical with me!"

Traveler: "Knock, knock!"

Knight: "Who's there?"

Traveler: "Ferdie!"

Knight: "Ferdie who?"

Traveler: "Ferdie last time, let me in!"

How do you know if a witch owns a vehicle?

It goes "Brrrrooooom, brrrooooom!"

I wanted to tell a time-traveling joke, but you guys didn't find it funny!

My friends told me I should try writing a book. Wow. What a novel idea!

The little mermaid saw two goldfish in the kingdom's tank. One of the goldfish asked her, "Princess! How do we drive this thing?"

Queen: "Knock, knock!"

Dwarf: "Who's there?"

Queen: "A bossy queen."

Dwarf: "A bo-"

Queen: "You should say 'a bossy queen who' now!"

Wendy: "Peter Pan is always flying, isn't he?"

Tinkerbell: "Yeah, he just Neverlands!"

What always follows a unicorn wherever she goes?

Her beautiful, sparkly tail!

What did the wizards get in trouble for?

Wand-ering around late!

How do unicorns and horses greet one another?

"Hey, neigh-bor!"

What did the monsters play during recess?

Swallow the Leader!

THE MOST TREASURED CUSTOMER YOU!

The Laughing Lion hopes you enjoyed the book!

As the Lion was writing it, he imagined how happy you'd be with the finished book.
How you'd jump for joy when you received it in the post.
How you'd write in your journal that it's the best book on the planet!
How you'd pass it onto your children for generations to come.

If you did enjoy the book, please take 20 seconds to leave a review.

The Laughing Lion loves reading all the happy moments his books spark.

Wishing you many more joyous moments!

Laughing Lion

Lightning Source UK Ltd.
Milton Keynes UK
UKHW021045231221
396109UK00003B/261

9 780995 884748